SAND

by
Ellen J. Prager
illustrated by
Nancy Woodman

NATIONAL GEOGRAPHIC SOCIETY
Washington, D.C.

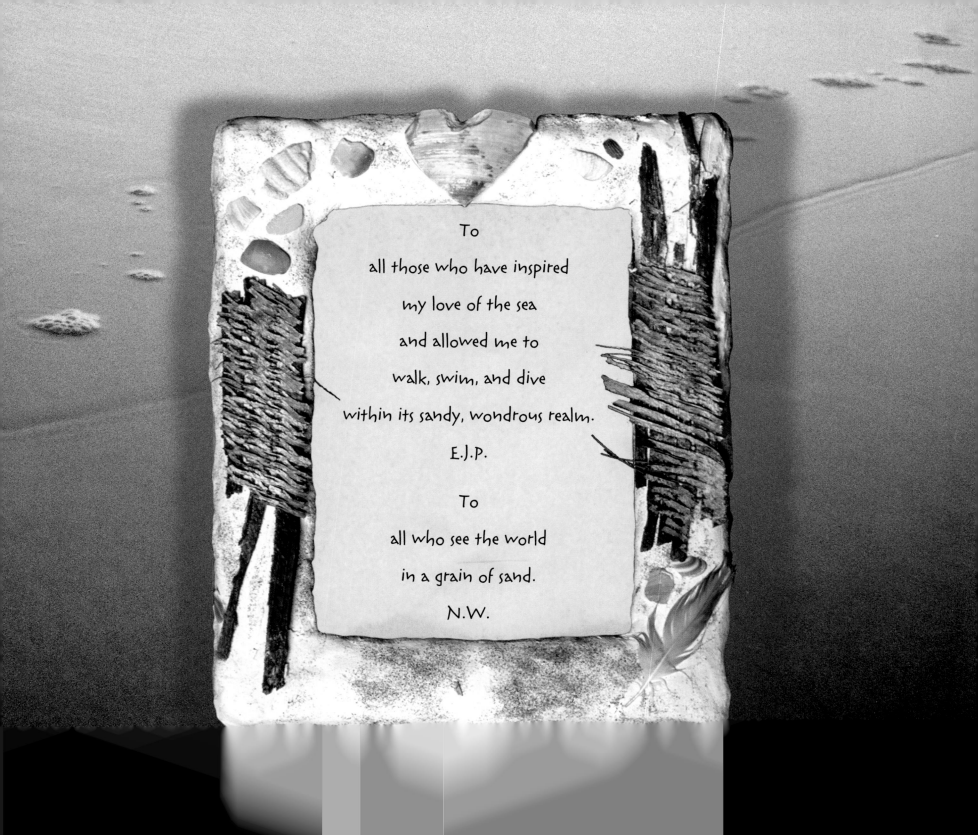

To

all those who have inspired

my love of the sea

and allowed me to

walk, swim, and dive

within its sandy, wondrous realm.

E.J.P.

To

all who see the world

in a grain of sand.

N.W.

Beaches are made of sand.
Desert dunes are made of sand.
Sand can be home to crabs and clams or seagulls and
stingrays. People like to walk on sand, lie on sand,
and build big sandcastles.

What is sand?
Where does sand come from?
And how does sand get to the ocean's edge
on a beach or piled high into a tall sand dune?
Let the sand sleuth show you the way!

We use the word SAND to describe the size of a grain.

Sand is made up of grains smaller than gravel but bigger than mud in size.

Gravel

Sand

Mud

Sand grains often come from
rocks that have been broken down into
smaller and smaller pieces over a very
long period of time. Sand can
also be made of small pieces of crystal,
shell, lava, or coral.

Red Sand

White Sand

Green Sand

Sand can be many colors—white, red, green, tan, or black. Some sand even looks like the black and white of a Dalmatian's spotted coat.

Tan Sand

Black Sand

Black-and-
White Sand

The color of sand comes from the color of its grains.

Sand made from coral and shells
forms the whitest of white beaches.

Waves crashing onto a coral reef bring bits and chunks of coral and shells to the beach and, over time, create sparkling white beaches along tropical shores.

Sometimes sand is made of crystals.
Crystals are made of minerals, and minerals come
from rocks. Crystals of different minerals form
sands of different colors.

Green sand is commonly made up of
small crystals of the mineral olivine.

Crystals of the mineral garnet can make sand look red.

One of the most common minerals found on land is quartz. Quartz crystals can be many colors—pink, gray, brown, white, or clear—and usually make sand look tan or off-white.

Many sands are made up of a mixture of grain types, including rock fragments, mineral crystals, and shell or coral pieces.

This spotted sand is made up of white coral pieces and black rock fragments.

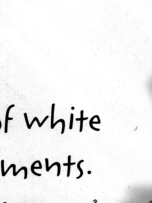

This colorful sand is a mix of red rock fragments and green crystals.

Quartz crystals and rock fragments make this sand look gray.

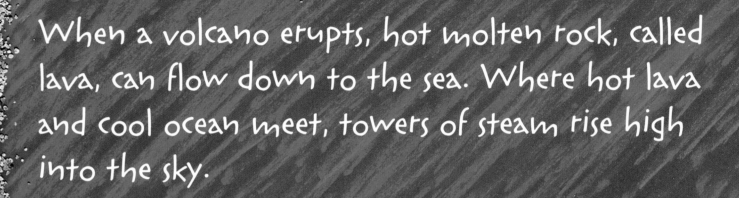

When a volcano erupts, hot molten rock, called
lava, can flow down to the sea. Where hot lava
and cool ocean meet, towers of steam rise high
into the sky.

Cool water turns the fiery red lava into hard black rock. Very quick cooling can cause the rock to shatter into small, shiny black pieces—instant black sand.

Now you know what sand looks like up close
and what it is commonly made of.
But how does sand get onto a beach or built
into a tall sand dune?

There are several different ways that sand can be moved from one place to another.

Water

Wind

Ice

Rivers can carry rocks from high in the mountains to faraway seashores.

As rocks are washed down toward the sea, they bump against each other, breaking down into smaller and smaller pieces—creating sand.

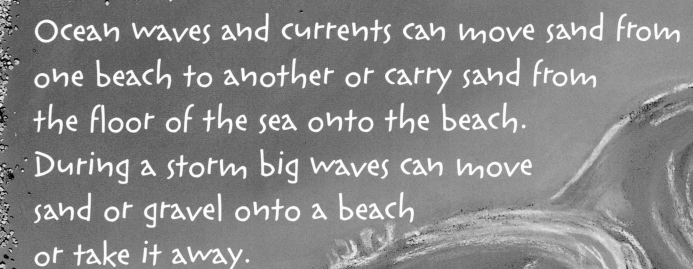

Ocean waves and currents can move sand from one beach to another or carry sand from the floor of the sea onto the beach. During a storm big waves can move sand or gravel onto a beach or take it away.

Sand grains on beaches that are pounded by big waves become round and shiny by bumping and rubbing against each other in the water.

Wind can pick up sand grains and create small ripples, like tiny waves on water, or build sand dunes as tall as buildings.

Sand grains that have been blown by the wind tend to have pointy sides and look frosted.

Ice can trap sand in its chilly grip and carry it to the sea. When the ice melts, the sand falls onto the land or into the water.

Sand, Sand, Sand

It comes in many colors but only
a few sizes. Remember, sand is
just a grain size: bigger than
mud but smaller than gravel.
If you look close, you might
see pieces of coral, shells,
or crystals in the sand.
Flowing water, blowing
wind, or moving ice
can break big rocks into
small pieces and bring
them to a beach where
wind can build tall dunes.

Next time you walk on a sandy beach, climb a high sand dune, or get ready to build a big sandcastle, bend down and scoop up a handful of sand.

What is it made of? How did it get there? Look for clues hidden in the grains to answer your questions!

SHAKE IT UP!

If you'd like to try and make some sand on your own, here's what you'll need....

An empty coffee can with a lid
A cup of clean water
3 or 4 small rocks (pebbles)
A clear plastic cup
A magnifier (optional)

1) Before starting the experiment, rinse out the coffee can and clean off the rocks so that there's no loose dirt on them.

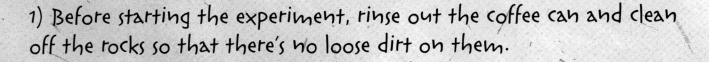

2) Place the rocks in the can and add the cup of water. Snap the lid on tight and get ready to shake, rattle, and roll!

3) Holding the can so that the lid is on top, shake the can with the rocks and water as hard as you can for about three minutes.
If you get tired, take a break and start again. You may even want to put on your favorite song to dance to while you're shaking.

4) After three minutes of shaking, carefully remove the lid from the can and pour some of the water into the clear plastic cup. How does the water look now? Why is it cloudy instead of clear? (Tiny pieces of rock broke off to make the water look dirty).

5) Take out the rocks and look at them closely. How have they changed?

6) Run your finger along the bottom of the can. Do you feel something rough and gritty? Look at the grit with a magnifier. Can you guess what you've made? SAND!

By shaking the can with the water and the rocks, you were just like the current in a river or the waves in the ocean. The moving water made the rocks hit together. Little by little small pieces chipped off to make sand. The longer you shake, the more sand you make!

If you want to make more sand, try using different types of rocks to see how the sand changes. You can even experiment by using some small pieces of shell or coral.

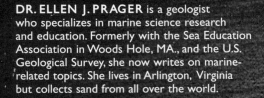

DR. ELLEN J. PRAGER is a geologist who specializes in marine science research and education. Formerly with the Sea Education Association in Woods Hole, MA., and the U.S. Geological Survey, she now writes on marine-related topics. She lives in Arlington, Virginia but collects sand from all over the world.

NANCY WOODMAN is the author-illustrator of *Sea-Fari Deep*, a book about exploring deep-sea hydrothermal vents, published by the National Geographic Society. She has illustrated ten other children's books. When not out sleuthing around, Nancy lives in Poulsbo, Washington, by the beach. She welcomes e-mail at nanneroo@aol.com.

Published by the
National Geographic Society
1145 17th Street N.W.
Washington, D.C. 20036

The artwork in this book is a digital collage of pastels on sand-paper, watercolors, and photographs. The photographs shown through the sandpiper sleuth's magnifying glass were taken through a microscope.

Book design by Nancy Woodman

Library of Congress Cataloging-in-Publication Data

Prager, Ellen J.
Sand / by Ellen J. Prager
p. cm.
Summary: Describes the formation of sand from materials such as coral, rock, or crystals and shows how it can be moved through water, wind, ice, and other erosion agents.
ISBN 0-7922-7104-1 (hardcover)
ISBN 0-7922-5583-6 (paperback)
[Sand—Juvenile Literature.] I. Woodman, Nancy, ill.
II. Title.
QE471.2.P7   2000
553.6'22—dc21   99-29943

Experiment written by Stephen M. Tomecek

First paperback printing 2006

Printed in the United States of America

One of the world's largest nonprofit scientific and educational organizations, the National Geographic Society was founded in 1888 "for the increase and diffusion of geographic knowledge." Fulfilling this mission, the Society educates and inspires millions every day through its magazines, books, television programs, videos, maps and atlases, research grants, the National Geographic Bee, teacher workshops, and innovative classroom materials. The Society is supported through membership dues, charitable gifts, and income from the sale of its educational products. This support is National Geographic's mission to increase global understanding and promote conservation of our planet through exploration, research, and education.